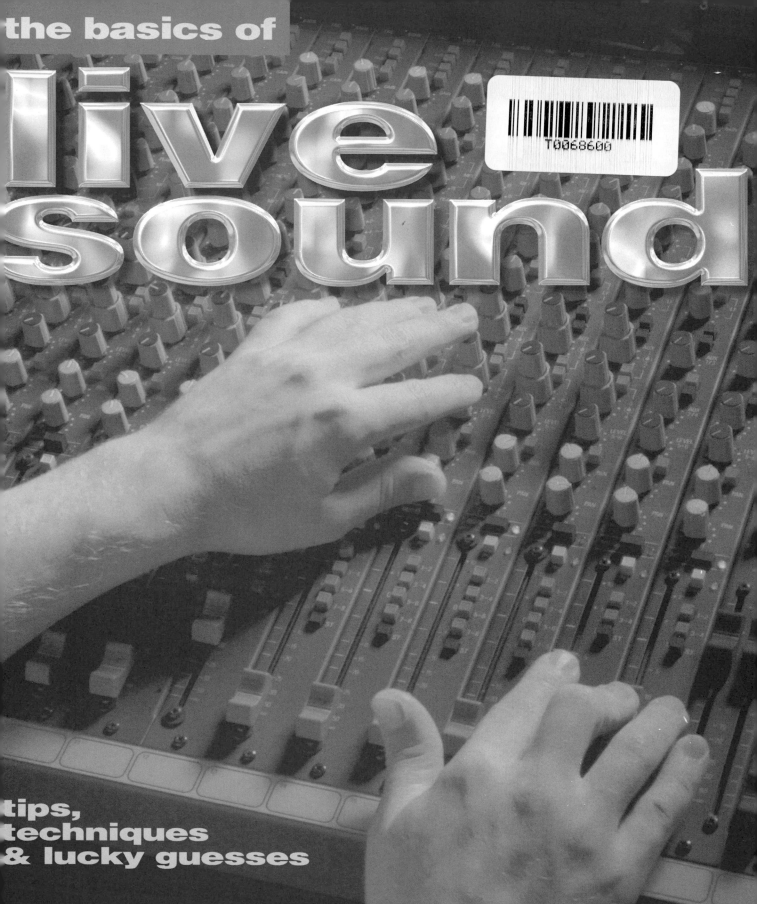

the basics of
live sound

tips, techniques & lucky guesses

jerry j. slone

T0068600

HAL•LEONARD®

ISBN 978-0-634-03028-4

7777 W. BLUEMOUND RD. P.O. BOX 13819 MILWAUKEE, WI 53213

Visit Hal Leonard Online at **www.halleonard.com**

contents

Acknowledgments 5

Introduction 7

Chapter 1 What Is a Sound Engineer? 9

Chapter 2 Sound and Hearing..11
    Sound Pressure Waves 11
    Frequency and Pitch 12

Chapter 3 Microphones 15
    Dynamic and Condenser Microphones..............................15
    Pick-up Patterns...18
        Cardioid...18
        Supercardioid..18
        Hypercardioid..19
        Omnidirectional..19
    Wireless Microphones...20
        Handheld and Lavalier 21
        Disadvantages of Wireless Microphones....................21

Chapter 4 Microphone Techniques 23
    Bass Drum 24
    Snare Drum and Toms..25
    Overhead Cymbals 26
    Hi-Hat Cymbals 27
    Electric Guitar Amplifier 28
    Piano (Acoustic) 29
    Violin/Fiddle (Acoustic) 30
    Acoustic Guitar/Bass Guitar/Keyboards 31
    Vocals..32

Chapter 5 Mixers 33
    Input...34
    Preamp and Attenuator 34
    Equalization...34
        Channel Equalization...34
        Filters...35
    Faders/Sliders...35

Chapter 6 Amplifiers...37

Chapter 7 Speakers 39
    Full-Range Speakers..40
    Crossovers...41

Chapter 8 The Audio Chain..43

Chapter 9 Tips and Advice...45

Appendix: Microphone Models and Specifications..........................47

Resources: Schools and Universities for Continuing Education 53

Glossary..57

acknowledgments

A heartfelt thanks to the following for their support: God; my wife Wendi; my two daughters, Madison and Phoenix; and all of my family members. Thanks also to my colleagues, all the folks at Hal Leonard Corporation, my former instructors at MTSU, David Turner, Tommy Waggoner, Riq Lazarus, Steve Fister, Bill Simmons, Tutti Westbrook and everyone at Fitzgerald-Hartley Management, Ralph Masterangelo, Kai Griffin, Peavey Electronics, Dan Majorie, Tim Lawrence, Joe Azar, Dean Hall, Trick Pony, The Kinleys, The Wilkinsons, Restless Heart, Doug Stone, Baillie & The Boys, Brady Seals, SHeDAISY, Shure Electronics, Sennheiser USA, Sound Check Rehearsal Studios, and all the wonderful musicians I've worked with and the friends I've made over the past years.

introduction

I finally convinced my parents to let me buy a drum kit when I was around the age of twelve. How they put up with all that noise, I'll never know, but will be forever grateful. All through Junior and Senior High School, my friends and I put together bands. We practiced almost every night, entered a lot of talent contests, and even won a few. For some reason, I was always the guy who got stuck hooking up our little PA and trying to tweak it to make it sound better—without much luck.

When I finally decided on which college to attend, I chose one that had very strong recording and music departments. I went to Middle Tennessee State University (MTSU), and enrolled in their Recording Industry program. While there, I studied everything from copyright law and artist management, to audio for motion pictures and Pro Tools software (an audio editing platform). I continued to perform with a couple of bands throughout college, and even played drums on some of the recording projects for other students. It was during my junior year of college that I began working for the MTSU Recording Department. I gave guided tours of the multi-million dollar John Bragg Mass Communications Building to prospective students from all over the world. This tour included an overview of two state-of-the-art digital recording studios, a fully integrated television studio, a remote recording truck, digital editing suites (audio and film), and a large electronic maintenance work area. I also helped students locate businesses that were seeking recording industry interns, and vice versa. In doing so, I made a lot of industry connections.

As soon as college ended for me, I had an offer to road manage and mix house audio for a regional blues-rock act, and spent the next two-and-a-half years touring with them. It didn't take me long to realize that many of the things that I was responsible for weren't covered in any class; so, much of my education came through hands-on experience. I also learned the value of flexibility and multi-tasking. I did it all—mixed sound, ran the lights, road managed, and sometimes drove the van that pulled a 12-foot U-Haul packed-to-the-gills with gear.

After I'd had enough of the college and club touring circuit, I pursued opportunities to work with major label recording acts. It wasn't long before I was able to do so, and still do so today. After years of reading books and magazines on sound-related topics—many of which made sense to me, but could be quite confusing to someone new to the subject—I decided to write about the basics of live sound myself; approaching it from the standpoint of a real beginner. Hopefully, the topics covered in this book have been presented in a manner simple enough to make sense, yet thorough enough to familiarize the beginner with its concepts and terminology. So, let's get started!

chapter 1

what is a sound engineer?

Have you ever gone to a concert and noticed the mixing board, with all of its flashing lights, buttons, knobs, and other electronic gizmos? Ever wonder what all of those buttons and knobs do? And what about that person standing at the board? Ever wonder who that person is and what exactly they're doing at that board? These are all questions I've heard before. Therefore, the first thing that we need to do is come up with a definition for a sound engineer.

A sound, or audio, engineer is a person who brings together separate sounds to create one sound. Sound engineers *mix*—adjust, enhance, combine, and blend—sounds together for such things as television commercials, radio station transmissions, and musical groups (live and in recording studios). A sound engineer mixing a live band, for example, would take all of the single musical sounds from the act—guitars, drums, keyboards, vocals—and combine them together so that all of the instruments are balanced in volume, and the singers can be heard clearly.

A live sound engineer also tries to recreate a natural representation of the sounds that he or she is mixing. In other words, they try to make a musical group sound integrated and cohesive—similar to how they would sound on a CD. One way that a sound engineer can do this is to change the EQ, or tone, of certain sounds that he or she is mixing. For example, if the engineer is having trouble distinguishing the low tones of the bass guitar from those of the bass drum, he or she can brighten, or add high frequencies to, the bass guitar in order to better distinguish its sound from the low frequencies of the bass drum. Another example is that when a lead vocalist sings more softly than normal (as singers often do during a slow part of a song) the engineer could turn up, or increase, the volume of the singer's voice so that it is not drowned-out by the other instruments. The engineer would then return the volume to its original setting when the slow part of the song is over.

Before we get into all of the different aspects of mixing live sound and the responsibilities of the live sound engineer, let's briefly go over a topic crucial to the fundamentals of live audio: sound and hearing.

chapter 2

sound and hearing

When a sound engineer mixes music, what he or she is really doing is taking different musical elements and combining them to create a unified, balanced mix of sounds; or sometimes, even a totally new musical episode. What we have to remember is that everyone perceives sound differently. The way our ears and brain interpret sound is truly amazing and detailed. So, without turning this into a book on anatomy, let's touch on the basics.

Sound Pressure Waves

Sound arrives to our ears by way of *sound pressure waves*—sonic waves created by the vibrations of a sound source that propagate, or travel, through the air. Someone's voice, a radio, or the hammer that strikes the strings of a piano are all sources of sonic vibrations. The characteristics of these waves—high pitch having short waves and low pitch having long waves—change as the *timbre*, or "color," of the sounds change. For example, the length of the sound waves created by someone blowing a whistle, which has a high pitch, would be much shorter than the waves created by someone playing a bass drum, which has a low pitch.

Figure 1

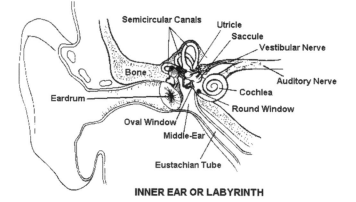

INNER EAR OR LABYRINTH

Once the sound pressure waves have reached the ear, they travel through the auditory, or ear, canal to the eardrum. The eardrum is a stretched, drum-like membrane that is sensitive to even the smallest vibrations from the slightest sound. The pressure of these waves causes the eardrum itself to vibrate, and these vibrations are then transmitted to the hammer, anvil, and stirrup. These three middle-ear bones act as both an *amplifier*, by strengthening the vibratory signals given to them by the eardrum, and a *limiting device*, by reducing the levels of loud and/or transient sounds. Sound waves then travel into the cochlea, or inner ear, which contains two fluid-filled chambers. Within these chambers are tiny hair receptors lined in rows. Vibrations are passed along to these hairs, which react to the different frequencies of the waves, producing the sensation of hearing. Hearing loss generally occurs either when these tiny hairs are damaged, or as they deteriorated with age.

Frequency and Pitch

Frequency and pitch are closely related. *Frequency* refers to the number of sound waves that pass a given point in unit time, and is measured in units of cycles per second called *Hertz* (Hz). Figure 2 shows the difference in the number of cycles that pass through a given point when a sound is of a high frequency and low frequency. *Pitch* is how the brain interprets the frequency of an emitted sound—heard as the highness or lowness of a tone. The average human ear can perceive frequencies, or pitches, from 20–20,000 Hz (or 20–20,000 cycles per second). For example, the foghorn of a ship, which we perceive as having a low pitch, also has a low-number frequency: about 80 Hz.

Figure 2

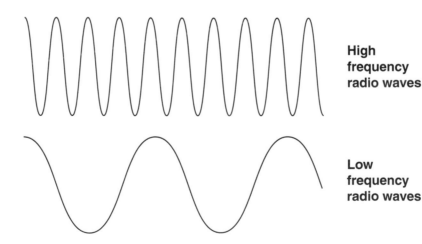

High frequency radio waves

Low frequency radio waves

The human ear is most sensitive to mid-range frequencies, which cause the bones of the ear to vibrate more intensely than high- or low-range frequencies. However, as the *level*, or perceived volume, of sound increases, we tend to hear the lower and higher frequencies at a perceived volume more equal to that of the mid-range frequencies. Figure 3 shows some frequencies related to everyday sounds.

Figure 3

Frequencies Related to Everyday Sounds

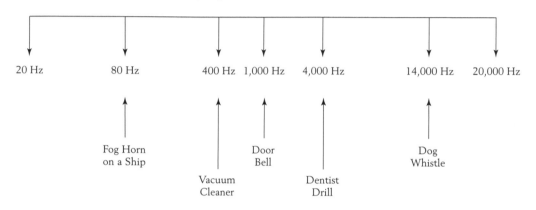

The *Sound Pressure Level* (SPL) is the pressure of sound vibration measured at a specific point. Both SPL and changes in signal level are measured in units of intensity called *decibels* (dB). Sound pressure decibels are usually measured with a *sound level meter* in units of dB SPL (decibels of sound pressure).

The louder, or more intense, the sound, the higher the sound pressure level. The average sound level of a spoken conversation is around 70 dB SPL; an average sound level of a home stereo is approximately 85 dB SPL. SPLs at or above 130 dB SPL are considered to have reached the *threshold of pain*—so loud that the ears hurt. Figure 4 shows the decibel levels for some common sounds.

Figure 4

SPL Levels Related to Everyday Sounds

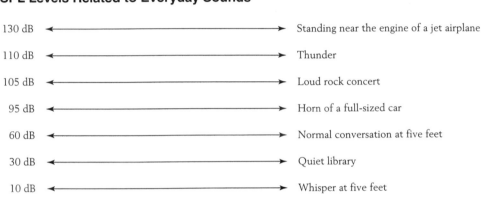

130 dB	Standing near the engine of a jet airplane
110 dB	Thunder
105 dB	Loud rock concert
95 dB	Horn of a full-sized car
60 dB	Normal conversation at five feet
30 dB	Quiet library
10 dB	Whisper at five feet

Having discussed the basics of how sound is received and perceived by the human ear, we're ready to move on to another sound-processing device: the microphone.

chapter 3
microphones

Now that we understand a little more about how the ear works, let's talk about the microphone, which is, in a sense, a type of an ear. Microphones essentially hear, capture, and relay sound to an electronic inner ear, such as a mixing board or an effects processor (audio gear that can dramatically alter the sound of an instrument or voice). Microphones are devices that change sound waves into *electrical impulses*, or signals. In order to satisfy the numerous applications necessary, and the personal preferences desired, there is a wide range of microphones available.

While there are many elements that make microphones different from one another, at the same time there are many elements that make most microphones similar. We are going to look at the most popular microphone types and discuss the different designs, pick-up patterns, and common uses of each. For more detailed information and per-model specifications of some of the most popular microphones used in live sound today, see the appendix at the back of this book.

Dynamic and Condenser Microphones

There are two basic microphone designs: *dynamic* and *condenser*. Without getting too complicated, let's examine how a microphone does what it does. We'll start by talking about the two types of dynamic microphones: moving coil and ribbon.

The most popular of the dynamic microphones are the *moving coil* types. Moving coil microphones do not require batteries or an external power supply, but are powered by *electromagnetic energy*—electrical energy that is generated when a conductive material moves within a magnetic field. In a moving coil microphone, the *conductor*—a substance, usually a metal, that allows the free flow of electrons—is a tightly wrapped coil of wire called a *voice coil*. This voice coil is attached to a thin Mylar diaphragm that is suspended in a magnetic field, and vibrates when hit by a sound wave. When the diaphragm vibrates, the attached voice coil is displaced, or moved, causing an electrical signal that is proportional to the particular characteristics—such as frequency or intensity—of the sound wave.

Ribbon microphones also use electromagnetic energy to create sound, but the diaphragm of these microphones is made from a very thin aluminum ribbon, as opposed to the Mylar diaphragm found in the moving coil designs. The ribbon microphone is not as popular as the moving coil type, due largely to the thinner, less durable diaphragm, which produces a much weaker output signal, and does not handle transient sounds or strong wind currents as well as the moving coil. Although new developments have been made in recent years to improve the performance and durability of ribbon microphones, the moving coil design remains the more popular of the two.

Figure 5

Dynamic Microphones

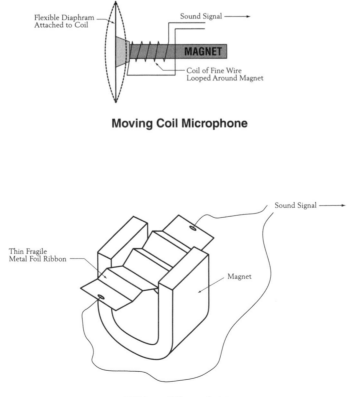

Moving Coil Microphone

Ribbon Microphone

The second type of microphone design is the *condenser* microphone. Unlike the dynamic microphone types, condenser microphones do require a supply of electricity, and therefore employ the principal of *electrostatic energy*—energy produced by an electrical charge. This charge usually comes from an external, or *phantom* power supply, such as an onboard battery or a mixing console. Condenser microphones consist of a membrane and a fixed plate (both conductive) that together act as a *capacitor*—a store for electrical energy. When sound pressure moves the membrane, a change in *capacitance*—the property that permits the storage of electricity when a potential difference exists between the two conductors—results in the output of electrical energy. Although less popular than the dynamic microphones, condenser mics are much lighter and can better handle noise.

Figure 6

Condenser Microphones

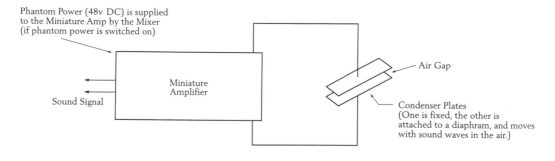

Phantom Power (48v DC) is supplied to the Miniature Amp by the Mixer (if phantom power is switched on)

Sound Signal

Miniature Amplifier

Air Gap

Condenser Plates (One is fixed, the other is attached to a diaphram, and moves with sound waves in the air.)

Pick-up Patterns

One of the most important characteristics about a microphone is its directionality, or *pick-up pattern*—essentially the area around the microphone that is sensitive to incoming sound. The most widely known pick-up patterns are cardioid, supercardioid, hypercardioid, and omnidirectional.

Cardioid

Figure 7 shows a diagram of the *cardioid*, or heart-shaped pick-up pattern of a moving coil microphone. Most vocal or speech situations can be best represented by the use of this microphone, as the car-

dioid's design is optimal for picking up sound in front of the microphone. This pick-up pattern also offers the best sound rejection at the rear of the mic, which is important for keeping unwanted noise out of the original sound source. Some popular microphones that use the cardioid pick-up pattern are the Shure SM57, Shure SM58, AKG D-112, and the Sennheiser MD 421.

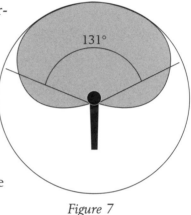

Figure 7

Supercardioid

Figure 8 shows a diagram of a *supercardioid* microphone. The pick-up pattern of a supercardioid is narrower than that of the cardioid, and it has the capability for some sound pick-up at the rear of the microphone. Like the cardioid, most vocal or speech situations can have wonderful results with a supercardioid pattern microphone. Some popular microphones that use this pick-up pattern are the Shure Beta 87, Shure Beta 98, Sennheiser ME 65, Audix OM-6, and the CAD-E100.

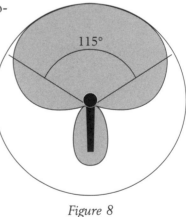

Figure 8

Hypercardioid

Figure 9 shows the pick-up pattern of a *hypercardioid* microphone, also referred to as a *figure-eight* pattern. Many of the more expensive microphones offer the ability to select the desired pick-up pattern, with the choices usually being cardioid, hypercardioid, or omnidirectional. The hyper-cardioid has an even narrower pick-up pattern than the supercardioid, but also has stronger sound pick-up at the rear of the microphone. This type of microphone is much more common in the recording studio than on stage, as it tends to have poor feedback rejection—which means less flexibility with microphone and monitor placement. Some popular microphones that allow pattern selection (including hypercardioid) are the Sure KS44, AKG C414, and the CAD E200.

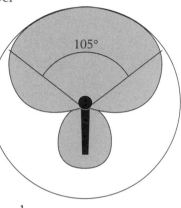

Figure 9

Omnidirectional

Figure 10 shows the pick-up pattern of an *omnidirectional* microphone, which—due to its 360-degree pick-up radius—picks up sound evenly in all directions. This type of microphone is commonly used for situations in which background noise, such as audience applause, is desired. Because these microphones are designed to pick up all surrounding sound, they are very susceptible to feedback.

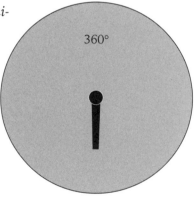

Figure 10

Wireless Microphones

A *wireless microphone* uses three components—an input device, a transmitter, and a receiver—instead of a cable to transfer sounds. The *input device* provides an audio signal that is sent by the *transmitter*, which converts the audio signal into a radio signal, and broadcasts it through an antenna. The *receiver* then picks up the transmitted radio signal and converts it back into an audio signal. The output of the receiver is the same as that of a standard microphone, thus allowing it to be connected to a typical microphone input in a sound system.

Most of today's wireless microphones operate in either *UHF* (ultra-high frequency) or *VHF* (very high frequency). One of the most notable differences between these two frequency spectra is that UHF radio waves are much shorter than VHF, which allows for the use of smaller antennae in both the transmitter and receiver of a wireless unit. The most economic difference between UHF and VHF wireless microphones is the relatively higher cost of manufacturing UHF equipment.

Figure 11

Wireless microphones are commonly used by a number of people. One of the most popular users of the wireless microphone is the stage performer. Performers sometimes prefer wireless microphones to cabled microphones because they provide more freedom to move around the stage without having to worry about tangling microphone cables.

Handheld and Lavalier

The two most popular types of wireless microphones are handheld microphones and Lavalier microphones. *Handheld wireless microphones* look like normal microphones except that, instead of a cable, it employs an antenna for signal transmission. *Lavalier microphones* are small microphones that are wired to a mini body-pack transmitter, which is usually clipped onto the neck or chest area of the wearer. Because of their inconspicuous and unobtrusive design, Lavalier microphones are often used in television broadcast situations.

Disadvantages of Wireless Microphones

Although wireless microphones offer more freedom on stage, and eliminate the need for crewmembers to weave cables around television props, etc., they also come with a few disadvantages. One disadvantage is *transmission loss*. It is difficult for a signal that is broadcast and received to equal the strength and integrity of that which is hard-wired. Often, *interference*—a disturbance from another source (such as a television or radio station) that obstructs, interrupts, or degrades signal transmission—can cause problems. In high-end wireless microphones, the user often has the ability to scroll through different frequencies and channel groups in order to find the strongest and cleanest signal available. This makes it easier for the touring performer to maintain a clear signal from city to city.

Dropout, or loss of signal, can be one of the most frustrating things when using a wireless microphone. This occurs most commonly when the transmitter is too far from the receiver, and can usually be corrected by moving the receiver and transmitter closer together. High-gain receiving antennae are available, and are often the solution for increasing the effectiveness of wireless microphones. These antennae provide a platform to increase the wireless microphone's transmission distance, and also resist interference from other sources.

Now that we have an understanding of the most popular microphone types, let's take a look at some of the basic miking techniques used for getting the best sounds possible, and the specific miking needs of various musical instruments.

chapter 4
microphone techniques

One of the most important factors in achieving good sound is proper microphone placement. Microphone techniques vary from engineer to engineer; some engineers are always willing to try new approaches, while others tend to be more conventional. This section is intended to give you a starting point; from this, feel free to move things around and see what happens. My theory is that there are many different ways to accomplish effective results.

Let's go over the main objectives of microphone selection and placement. First and foremost, we are trying to maximize the pick-up of the natural sound of an instrument or vocal. Second, we want to minimize *background noise*, or the pick-up of undesired sound from other instruments. Finally, we want to maximize *gain-before-feedback*—the amount of *headroom* (the capacity of a device to peak without distortion) a sound system has before the output level is great enough to produce feedback. As this is an important concept for attaining good sound quality, let's go over it in more detail.

Absolute gain—the highest gain in volume achievable before feedback occurs—is determined by the physical difference between the microphone and the speakers of a sound system. In other words, if a sound system is operated below the absolute gain, feedback will never occur; if the gain controls of the system are turned up, the absolute gain will eventually be exceeded and feedback will occur. When feedback does occur, increasing the original level into the microphones—so that the louder signal is amplified—allows the overall volume of the system to be turned down. Also, getting closer to the microphone will increase the volume going into the microphone, allowing the overall system to be turned down—discouraging the "feedback monster."

Now we're ready to discuss microphone placement techniques. Let's start with the miking of a drum kit. Since a drum kit consists of several different components, we have the opportunity to play around quite a bit. Always try to start with well-sounding, well-tuned instruments. Remember, a sound engineer can improve the sound only so much, especially if the source of the sound itself is poor. With that said, let's check out the miking of a bass drum.

Bass Drum

The bass, or kick, drum is usually the heart of a live mix. It's hard to get into the feel and intensity of the band if the bass drum isn't happening. This is evident in a rock band, for example, as all of the other instruments depend on the bass drum to build the foundation for the song. A good starting position for a bass drum microphone is as follows:

- Place the microphone inside the drum, about one-third of the way between the front and rear of the drum.

- Aim the microphone at the center of the drumhead. If the drum has a front head, make sure that the microphone, mic stand, and mic cable do not touch the front head. This could create an unnatural drum sound.

- Move the microphone closer to the beater head to produce more of a "click" in the drum sound. Move the microphone closer to the front head to produce a "rounder," or more "beefy" sound.

It usually helps the sound of a bass drum if there is some sort of muffling in the drum. Something like a towel or a small pillow works best. Make sure the front and the beater head of the drum share the muffling materials.

Figure 12

Snare Drum and Toms

A good starting place for snare drum and tom miking is as follows:

- Start with the microphone about two inches from the drum, and aim it just over the hoop of the drum—at about a 45-degree angle (See figure 13). It is important not to get the microphone too close to the top drum head, as this will create more of a dull "thud" instead of a nice "pop" from the drum.

- Be careful not to put too much space between the drum and the microphone, as this may allow it to pick up other unwanted sounds, such as the bass drum or hi-hat cymbals.

- Always keep the microphone clear of the drummer, so that it doesn't take a hit from a drumstick.

Figure 13

A good choice for snare drum miking is the moving coil microphone. For many years the industry standard has been the Shure SM57.

Overhead Cymbals

Mike overhead cymbals as follows:

- Using two boom microphone stands, place condenser microphones about two feet over the cymbals. The mics should be spaced two to three feet apart (see Figure 14).

- The microphones should be pointed down towards the cymbals. If you have two cymbals on one side of the drum kit, aim the microphone between the two.

Figure 14

A recommended condenser microphone for cymbals would be a set of Shure KSM32's.

Hi-Hat Cymbals

Mike hi-hat cymbals as follows:

- Use a condenser microphone with *low-frequency roll-off*—attenuation, or trim, of the lower frequencies—and place it about four to six inches above the outside edge of the hi-hat, aiming down (see Figure 15).

- Be careful about picking up too much of the snare drum or other drums when miking the hi-hat.

Figure 15

A popular microphone for hi-hat miking is the Shure SM81.

Electric Guitar Amplifier

Mike an electric guitar amplifier as follows:

- Place the microphone about two to four inches from the speaker cone, slightly off-center (see Figure 16).

- To increase the bass frequencies, place the microphone closer.

- For a brighter tone, place the microphone near the center of the speaker cone.

- For a softer tone, place the microphone near the edge of the speaker cone.

Figure 16

The most popular microphone choice for electric guitar amplifiers is the dynamic (moving coil) microphone. Again, the Shure SM57 is a popular choice.

Piano (Acoustic)

Mike an acoustic piano as follows:

- First, raise or remove the lid of the piano.

- Use two microphones—one over the bass strings and one over the treble strings.

- Place the microphones about six inches over the bass and treble strings, and about six inches horizontally from the hammers (see Figure 17).

Figure 17

Condenser microphones are generally preferred for miking a piano. Placing the microphones too close to the piano strings will prevent you from capturing the fullness of the piano's sound. Move the microphones around until you get the most natural-sounding results.

Violin/Fiddle (Acoustic)

Mike a violin or fiddle as follows:

• Start with the microphone about eighteen inches over the top of the instrument; adjust accordingly (see Figure 18).

• The most efficient way to get a violin into a live mix is by either using a direct (DI) box (see more under Acoustic Guitar/Bass Guitar/Keyboards, on page 31), or by running the violin though an amplifier and placing a microphone on the amp. A violin pickup is required for both techniques. Mike the amplifier just as you would an electric guitar amp.

Figure 18

Acoustic Guitar/Bass Guitar/Keyboards

The most common way to get an acoustic guitar or keyboard into the PA is thru the use of a *direct box* or *DI*—an interfacing device used to convert output from instruments, amplifiers, etc., into microphone output for input at the mixer (see Figure 19). If a direct box is used for acoustic guitar, a pickup will be needed. There are two types of DI boxes: active and passive. *Active* DI's require external, or *phantom*, power; they also commonly *color*, or alter, the audio signal in some way. *Passive* DI's are less expensive, and usually don't affect the timbre of your audio signal. A direct box is needed because the signal out of an acoustic guitar or keyboard is *unbalanced* and *high-impedance*, and most professional mixing consoles have *balanced* inputs and tolerate *low-impedance* input. Therefore, the direct box acts as a kind of a converter that takes the unbalanced, high-impedance input from the instrument and converts it to a balanced, low-impedance output.

Figure 19

This is also a very common method for getting a bass guitar in the mix as well. You could put a microphone on the bass amplifier, but taking a direct input from the bass amp to the board will help to clean up the mix. It's best to have as few open microphones on stage as possible.

Vocals

For lead vocalists, a good-quality, unidirectional (cardioid, supercardioid) microphone should be placed so that it just touches the vocalist's lips, or be only an inch or so away.

Remember that unidirectional microphones have a proximity effect that increases the bass response of the microphone as it gets closer to the sound source. If this bass response becomes too much, you can *roll off*—reduce the signal level—of the bass frequencies at the mixing board. Also, remind the vocalist to never cover the capsule, or head, of the microphone with the hands while singing, as this can create a very unnatural-sounding vocal.

Now that we've discussed microphones and miking techniques, let's examine the device through which sound passing through microphones is joined, processed, and refined: the mixer.

chapter 5
mixers

The main purpose of a mixer is to bring together all of the audio signals and combine them. There are as many options available for sound mixers as there are options for cars. A good mixer will have useable features and a nice practical layout, as well as the ability to accurately reproduce audio signals without *electronic coloration*—audible alterations arising from the *response pattern* (the way a microphone accentuates or de-emphasizes frequencies) of a microphone or loudspeaker.

Figure 20

The following are vital features of all mixers:

Input

A mixer's *input*—the section that receives the signal from the microphone, effects processor, amplifier, etc.—usually has two connection types: the first being a 1/4-inch phone connector, which accommodates musical instrument cables; and the other an *XLR*, which is for microphone cables.

Preamp and Attenuator

Due to the variances in audio signal volume, mixers come equipped with mechanisms such as a *preamp*—a device that amplifies, or increases, the volume of a signal—and/or an *attenuator*, or *trim*—a device that trims, or reduces the volume of a signal. The preamp could be thought of as a mixer's floodgate, as it helps to increase the *signal-to-noise ratio* (the ratio of the average signal to the background noise), thus improving the quality of audio. If a weak signal occurs, the preamp can boost the level up to a usable one without adding noise or hiss. If a signal is too strong, the trim can be used to reduce the level to a useable one. Without this inhibitor, the strong signal could cause distortion.

Equalization

There are as many opinions on how to use *equalization*, or *EQ*—the increasing or decreasing of frequency ranges through the use of tone controls, equalizers, or filters—in live audio as there are live audio sound engineers. Some engineers prefer to use EQ to add sparkle to their sound; others use it solely as a corrective device to control feedback. Take the time to practice and experiment with an equalizer. Learn how an EQ affects particular sounds. Learn when to EQ when not to EQ; then trust your ears to tell you which, and how much, EQ you really need.

Channel Equalization

Channel equalization is basically a way to change the tone of the individual audio signal coming into a particular channel of the mixer. There are three main types of channel EQ: shelving, peaking, and parametric. *Shelving EQ* refers to the rise and drop in frequency response at a selected frequency, which tapers off to a preset level, or shelf, and continues at this level to the end of the audio spectrum. *Peaking EQs* have a selectable *bandwidth*—the overall range of frequencies covered by a driver or a network—and will either boost or cut a certain number of decibels around a center frequency. This type of EQ is most commonly used to change mid-frequencies. With a *parametric EQ*, you have the ability to select the desired centered-frequency with a sweep control. It also includes a Q—a control that allows the adjustment of the bandwidth. Unlike a peaking EQ, which covers the area of an octave, the Q control can narrow or broaden that bandwidth, which gives greater control over changing the signal.

Filters

High pass and *low pass* filters are other examples of EQs. This type of equalizer allows certain frequencies to pass normally, while others are attenuated. If a mixing board has a low pass filter of 100 Hz, then all frequencies above 100 Hz are passed, while the frequencies of 100Hz and lower are processed. High pass filters work similarly.

Always remember to use equalization carefully. It can be easy to overuse EQ, which could result in unnatural sounds. EQ can also add noise. Keep in mind that an acoustic guitar should sound like an acoustic guitar.

Faders/Sliders

The *faders*, or *sliders*, of a mixing board are generally located near the bottom of the board. Each fader is a master volume control for what is being sent into the main outputs for that channel. It is a good idea to set the faders to the zero mark, and adjust the preamp as necessary, in order to achieve proper *gain structure*—the interconnectedness of audio equipment components, and the amount of amplification and attenuation that is performed by each component. (Remember that gain is the amount of sound that an individual preamp channel is receiving; *faders* control the amount of sound delivered to the output groups).

Now let's take a look at the component through which the sound from the mixer is sent: the amplifier.

chapter 6
amplifiers

The primary function of an *amplifier* is to power, or drive, loudspeakers. Amps are the energy source of a PA. A signal travels from either a microphone or a DI box into a mixer, then out of the mixer into a power amplifier, and finally to a speaker or speakers.

Figure 21

Power amplifiers appear in three major forms:

1. Built into a complete unit with a speaker (a musical instrument amplifier).

2. Built into a sound mixing board.

3. Independent units (most common for sound reinforcement).

A power amp should be able to reproduce input signals with little or no *coloration*, or alteration of sound. A quality amplifier will be able to accurately reproduce frequencies that are audible to the human ear (20–20,000Hz).

Qualities to Look for When Purchasing a Power Amp

- Total Harmonic Distortion (THD) — When a power amp is at full power, there is a small variance between the output signal and the input signal. Because of this, *harmonic*, or *ghost tones* (forms of distortion) are produced by the amplifier, and can be detected by the human ear (if the total amount of these tones exceeds one-percent of the total audio being heard). Always look for an amp with low harmonic distortion.

- Signal-to-Noise — All electronic equipment has a certain level of self-noise. Since there is no way to remove this, you should look for musical equipment with a very low noise floor. It is favorable to have the musical level much greater than the noise signal, so that the noise is unnoticeable. Always shop for equipment with a low signal-to-noise ratio.

- Slew Rate — The *slew rate* of an amplifier refers to how fast the amplifier responds to an input signal. An amp that can recover more quickly from an input signal will be more efficient. The faster the slew rate, the better.

- Circuitry Protection — Always look for protective devices when buying equipment. Short-circuit protectors and overheating protectors can save you a lot of money in repair bills.

We are now ready to go over the audio components to which sound from the amplifier is sent: the speakers.

chapter 7
speakers

Every loudspeaker converts electrical energy to acoustical energy, thus making it a *transducer*. Speakers use the principles of magnetism to convert this energy. A magnet has two opposite forces within itself: a positive and a negative pole. Poles that are alike oppose each other, while unlike poles attract. Speakers use a fixed, permanent magnet and an electromagnet, which is movable. The electromagnetism occurs as current flows through a coil of wire to create a positive magnetic field. These two magnetic fields oppose each other, causing the speaker to move away from the magnet. When the current changes directions, it causes the speaker to move in the opposite direction. This coil of wire is attached to a paper cone; as the coil moves, it causes the paper cone to move in a pumping motion.

A loudspeaker has several individual components that work together to make it a speaker. Let's go over a few of these components:

- Basket — The framework for all of the speaker's components. Most of the top-of-the-line models use an aluminum alloy for the basket, as this material is lightweight and does not interfere with the movements of the speaker's magnet.

- Cone — Employed in some speaker designs; usually made of paper or some type of synthetic, or plastic-like, material. The cone moves back and forth, moving air, and is glued to the voice coil, securing it.

- Dust Cover/Cap — Protects the voice coil from dust and dirt, and is usually made from paper, plastic, or aluminum.

- Magnet — A component involved in the generation of a speaker's magnetic field. The size of a speaker's magnet determines the strength of the magnetic field—the larger the magnet, the more efficient the speaker. Because efficiency is related to magnet size, the more efficient, top-of-the-line speakers usually cost more.

- Spider — The component that connects the cone to the basket. The spider is made with pleats, or folds, that allow the pumping action of the speaker to occur without causing any undue stress to the cone.

- Vent — The opening in the back of the magnet assembly that allows for the release of pressure that builds up, due to the moving of the voice coil under the dust cover/cap.

- Voice Coil — The aluminum or copper wire that winds around a cylinder made of plastic, paper, or aluminum. Since copper is a better conductor than aluminum, it is often favored in speaker design.

Full-Range Speakers

The perfect speaker would be able to reproduce all frequencies from 20–20,000 Hz equally; however, this is not possible from a single speaker. Speakers therefore come in all sizes. The size of the speaker usually dictates what area of frequencies it can produce more efficiently. As a general rule, smaller speakers are better at reproducing high frequencies (high-pitch tones), and larger speakers are better at reproducing lower frequencies (low-pitch tones). This is why many speaker cabinets combine different-sized speakers. For example, a full-range speaker cabinet may contain a 15-inch speaker to create the low (bass) sounds; a 12-inch speaker for the mid-range sounds; and some type of *driver*—a loudspeaker unit consisting typically of electromagnetic components, such as a magnet and voice coil, that feeds sound pressure waves into a horn—for the high frequencies. This way, frequencies can be represented equally.

A *cone driver*—a speaker in which the voice coil is attached to a cone that moves back and forth—is only one example of a driver used to generate sound. The other most common driver is called a *compression driver*. In short, a compression driver uses a similar design approach as a cone driver, except that there is a diaphragm, instead of a cone, attached to a voice coil. Compression drivers tend to be more efficient than cone drivers.

Another type of driver is the *piezo tweeter*, which uses a small crystal attached to a small diaphragm. Piezo tweeters are used only to reproduce high frequencies.

Crossovers

A *crossover*— a device that separates an audio signal into two or more frequency ranges—is the most common way to make a full-range speaker cabinet. By having a crossover, certain frequencies are directed to certain speakers or drivers. In our earlier example of a full-range speaker, a crossover would send the low frequencies to the 15-inch speaker, the mid-range to the 12-inch speaker, and the highs to the piezo tweeter.

There are two types of crossovers: passive and active. A *passive* crossover is a simple network of devices, usually located between the power amplifier and the speaker drivers; and is often located inside the speaker cabinet itself. Since passive crossovers are inserted *after* the power amplifier, a certain amount of level loss (loss of the pre-amplified signal) will occur, due to the insertion of this network of capacitors, resistors, etc., between the power amplifier and the speaker drivers.

Figure 22

Active, or electronic, crossovers are inserted *before* the power amplifier. Active crossovers are far more efficient than passive crossovers, because they operate at a fraction of the signal level at which a passive crossover operates. Since active crossovers work before the power amplifier to divide frequency ranges, a separate power amplifier must be used for each individual driver. For example, a two-way loudspeaker with an active crossover and two power amplifiers (or at least two separate channels of power) is called a *bi-amped* system. Likewise, a three-way loudspeaker with an active crossover and three power amplifiers (or at least three separate channels of power) is called a *tri-amped* system.

Figure 23

Bi-amplified or tri-amplified systems offer several performance advantages over conventional systems—the most important probably being that of more *headroom*. Audio programs, or music, are made up of many different frequencies and *harmonic frequencies*— frequencies derived from integral multiple(s) of the fundamental, or first harmonic, frequency (i.e. the second harmonic is twice the fundament frequency, the third harmonic is three times the fundamental frequency, etc.). Most of the energy from a power amplifier is used to generate low frequencies, with very little energy needed to generate high frequencies. When high and low frequencies are present, the lower frequencies can use up most of the power, with little or no power left for the highs. This can cause the power amp to *clip*, or distort, the signal. In a bi- or tri-amped system, a smaller amplifier can be used for the highs, while another amplifier can be designated for the lows—this with the help of the active crossover.

Having covered the topics of microphones, miking techniques, mixers, amplifiers, and speakers, let's put it all together by detailing the flow of sound through the audio chain.

chapter 8
the audio chain

The following will serve as a very simple outline depicting the flow of an audio signal. We'll start from the source and follow it through each of the stages until the point where it would be heard coming through a speaker. There are all kinds of physical and mechanical changes that a signal undergoes before it is picked up and heard by the ears.

Again, without turning this into a physics class, below is a simple example of the audio chain.

1. Source to microphone — A Blues performer standing on stage sings the line "woke up this mornin'." The sound travels from the performer's mouth and into a microphone.

2. Microphone to mixer — The signal travels through the microphone and its cable, then into the sound mixer.

3. Mixer to power amplifier — Once the signal reaches the mixer, it can be changed in several ways: it can be increased in gain, have some high frequencies added by the EQ, etc. As dictated by the fader settings, the signal is then sent out to the power amplifiers.

4. Power amplifier to speakers — Now that the signal has undergone the proper changes at the mixer, the amplifiers will increase the gain, or volume, and send it out to the loudspeaker.

5. Speakers to audience — The speakers reproduce the line "woke up this mornin'." This causes the audience, who is listening to the show, to get up and bust-a-move on the dance floor!

chapter 9
tips and advice

The most important advice that I would give an up-and-coming live sound engineer is to attempt to reproduce the sounds that are going into the system as accurately as possible.

I would also tell them to not be afraid to ask questions. If something doesn't make sense, ask. Never assume or guess, because that could result in a lost gig or damaged gear. Often, the engineer from the opening act will ask me questions about my mix, microphone choices, or techniques. I enjoy sharing information with others; and I too, will ask engineers about their techniques. One thing I've learned over the years is that the engineers who are sincere about what they do will usually take the time to answer questions from other engineers. Talking about different ways of mixing, microphone choices, etc., can be a great way to learn and get new ideas. Remember, there are as many different ways of doing things as there are engineers.

Also, be prepared to get plenty of criticism from others. The important thing to remember here is that people perceive sounds differently. Always listen to what others are saying, and try to make sense of it. Many times, people just want to have an input about something they know nothing about; but sometimes, valid critiquing can be very educational. It's important to keep a level head, cool temper, and an open mind when mixing. Patience can be an invaluable commodity. Also, I would have to discourage any drinking, drugs, etc., while mixing, as this can impair your judgment and your ability to hear accurately.

Being courteous is also very important. I am a strong believer in the rule that you will catch more flies with honey than vinegar. If you are in a situation where you are mixing your friend's band at a local nightclub, and your friend's guitar amp seems too loud to you, be tactful in how you ask him to turn it down. Explain to him why it needs to be lower in volume. Doing so could make your job a lot easier. Respect the musicians and the other engineers that you work with, and they will likely respect you as well.

Do me a favor, will you? Have fun doing this stuff. Whether you are just starting out or have years of experience, if you have fun it will show in the quality of your work. I've been working as a live sound engineer for years, and I will no longer take a tour or gig if it doesn't sound like fun. Remember, this isn't rocket science—enjoy yourself. I hope that something in this book will help you to do just that.

appendix:
microphone models and specifications

Shure SM57

The Shure SM57 is one of the most versatile and commonly used microphones on the planet. It has long been a standard on stage, as well as in the recording studio. The general characteristics of a SM57 are:

- Contoured frequency response for clean, instrumental reproduction and uniform voice control.

- Professional-quality reproduction for drums, percussion, and instrument amplifier miking.

- Uniform cardioid pick-up pattern isolates the main sound source while reducing background noise.

- Pneumatic shock-mount system cuts down handling noise.

- Frequency response of 40–15,000 Hz.

Shure SM58

For years the Shure SM58 and Beta 58 have been the vocal microphone choice of many artists and live sound engineers. This microphone is built to withstand the rigors of the touring musician, while providing a smooth, accurate reproduction of the human voice. The general characteristics of a SM58 are:

- Frequency response tailored for vocals, with brightened mid-range and bass roll-off.

- Uniform cardioid pick-up pattern isolates the main sound source and minimizes background noise.

- Pneumatic shock-mount system cuts down handling noise.

- Effective, built-in spherical wind and pop filter.

- Cardioid (unidirectional) dynamic.

- Frequency response: 50–15,000 Hz.

Shure Beta 58

AKG D-112

The AKG D-112 is a cardioid microphone tailored for use in reproducing low frequencies, such as those from a bass drum or bass guitar amplifier. This microphone is very rugged in design, and provides a punchy sound.

D112	
FREQUENCY RANGE	20 Hz to 17 kHz
POLAR PATTERN	Cardioid
SENSITIVITY	1.8 mV/Pa (–55dBV)
IMPEDANCE	210 ohms
SIZE	150 x 70 x 115 mm (5.9 x 2.8 x 4.5 in)
NET/SHIPPING WEIGHT	320/990 g (11.3 oz/2.2 lbs)

AKG D-112

C 414 B-ULS

The following is a specifications summary of the C 414 B-ULS:

C 414 B-ULS	
FREQUENCY RANGE	20 Hz to 20 kHz
POLAR PATTERNS	Cardioid, Hypercardioid, Omnidirectional and Figure-8
PREATTENUATION	–10 dB, –20 dB switchable
BASSCUT FILTER	12 dB/octave roll-off at 75 Hz or 150 Hz
SENSITIVITY	12.5 mV/Pa (–38dBV) (all patterns)
IMPEDANCE	180 ohms
EQUIVALENT NOISE LEVEL	14 dB-A
MAXIMUM SPL FOR 0.5% THD	140 dB (160dB@ –20dB) at 1 kHz 134 dB (154dB@ –20dB) 30Hz to 20Hz
POWER REQUIREMENT	9-48 V phantom power to DIN 45596
CURRENT CONSUMPTION	approx. 2 mA
SIZE	141 x 45 x 35 mm (5.6 x 1.8 x 1.4 in.)

C414 B-ULS

AKG C414

This microphone has been continuously improved and updated. Features like selectable pick-up patterns, pads, or low-frequency attenuation make it an ideal tool for difficult recording situations in the studio, as well as on the road.

Some of the specifications of the AKG C414 are:

- Cardioid pick-up pattern.

- 30–17,000 Hz frequency response.

- 2 mV/Pa +/- 3 dB sensitivity (free field, no load) (1 kHz)

- 200 ohms; nominal impedance.

AKG C414

MD 421

The MD 421 is one of the best-known microphones in the world. Its excellent sound qualities enable it to cope with the most diverse recording conditions and broadcasting applications. The five-position bass control enhances its all-round qualities.

MD 421

ND868

Electro-Voice N/D868

The Electro-Voice N/D 868 is a cardioid microphone designed specifically for use with kick drums. Its extended, low frequency response is ideal for tightening live and studio mixes.

resources:

schools and universities for continuing education

The following is a list of universities and schools that offer courses in music production, recording, and business-related topics of the music industry. This information was compiled through research, and should be double-checked with each facility to ensure accuracy.

These schools offer different degree programs, areas of emphasis, and required term-lengths. They range from six-week quickies, to four-year undergraduate programs, to graduate-level options. The best way to decide which school or program is right for you is to start by asking yourself these questions:

1. What do I want to do?

2. What training do I need to be qualified for the area I want to work in?

3. What can I afford to spend on this training?

Once you have answered these three questions, you're on the right track to narrowing the selection.

This is only a small list of the schools available; check your area for others. Unless otherwise noted, Bachelor Degree programs are typically four-year programs, Associate Degree programs require two-years, and Certificate programs vary in length from a few weeks to one year.

Eastern Schools

Berklee College of Music
1140 Boylston Street
Boston MA, 02215
Phone: 617-747-0084
Website: www.berklee.edu
Degrees/Certificates: Bachelor of
Music Degree.

Belmont University
1900 Belmont Blvd.
Nashville, TN 37212
Phone: 615-460-5504
Website: www.schlbus.belmont.edu
Degrees/Certificates: Bachelor's
Degree in Business Administration,
with four areas emphasizing music
business.

Full Sail Recording Arts
3300 University Blvd.
Winter Park, FL 32792
Phone: 407-679-0100
Website: www.fullsail.com
Degrees/Certificates: Associate of
Science, Recording Arts.

Middle Tennessee State University
P.O. Box 21
Murfreesboro, TN 37132
Phone: 615-898-2578
Website: www.mtsu.edu
Degrees/Certificates: Bachelor of
Science in Recording Industry, with
emphasis in Production Technology
or Music Business.

Nassau Community College
One Education Drive
Garden City, NY 11530
Phone: 516-572-7446
Website: www.sunnynassau.edu
Degrees/Certificates: Certificate in
Studio Recording Technology (one-
year program).

Barton College
Barton College Station
Wilson, NC 27893
Phone: 800-345-4973
Website: www.barton.edu
Degrees/Certificates: Bachelor of
Science Degree in Recording
Technology.

Central Schools

Houston Community College
1060 West Sam Houston Pkwy.
North
Houston, TX 77043
Phone: 713-718-5621
Website: www.hccs.cc.tx.us/nwcol-
lege/audit/main.htm
Degrees/Certificates: Certificate in
Audio Engineering (one-year pro-
gram), Certificate in Video
Production (one-year program), and
Associates (A.A.S.) Degree in Audio
Engineering (two-year program).

Cleveland Institute of Music
11021 East Blvd.
Cleveland, OH 44106
Phone: 216-791-5000
Website: www.cim.edu
Degrees/Certificates: Bachelor of
Music in Audio Engineering.

Columbia College Chicago
600 South Michigan
Chicago, IL 60605
Phone: 312-482-9068
Website: www.colum.edu
Degrees/Certificates: Bachelor of
Arts Degree with a major in Sound
Technology.

University of Wisconsin, Oshkosh
Music Department
800 Algoma Blvd.
Oshkosh, WI 54901
Phone: 920-424-4224
Website: www.uwosh.edu
Degrees/Certificates: Bachelor of
Music, with emphasis in Recording
Technology.

The Recording Workshop
455 Massieville Rd.
Chillicothe, OH 45601
Phone: 800-848-9900
Website:
www.recordingworkshop.com
Degrees/Certificates: Certificate in
Recording Engineering and Music
Production (five-week program).

Northeast Community College
801 East Benjamin Ave.
Norfolk, NE 68702
Phone: 402-644-0506
Website: www.northeastaudio.org
Degrees/Certificates: Associate
Degree in Audio Recording.

Western Schools

Art Institute of Seattle
2323 Elliott Ave.
Seattle, WA 98121
Phone: 800-275-2471
Website: www.ais.edu
Degrees/Certificates: Associate of
Applied Arts in Audio Production.

Audio Institute of America Audio
Recording School
814 46th Ave.
San Francisco, CA 94115
Phone: 415-752-0701
Website: www.audioinstitute.com
Degrees/Certificates: Diploma in
Recording Engineering

Conservatory of Recording Arts &
Sciences
2300 East Broadway Rd.
Tempe, AZ 85282-1707
Phone: 800-562-6383
Website: www.audiorecord-
ingschool.com
Degrees/Certificates: Master
Recording Program

Los Angeles Recording Workshop
5278 Lankershim Blvd.
North Hollywood, CA 91601
Phone: 818-763-7400
Website: www.idt.net/~larw
Degrees/Certificates: Recording
Engineer Certificate and Audio-
Video Production Certificate (both
seven-month programs).

Mt. San Jacinto College
1499 North State St.
San Jacinto, CA 92583
Phone: 909-487-6752 x1577
E-mail: music@msjc.cc.ca.us
Degrees/Certificates: Audio
Technologies Certificate (eighteen
units); Associate Degree in Audio
Technologies

Sound Master Recording Engineer
School Audio/Video Institute
10747 Magnolia Blvd.
North Hollywood, CA 91601
Phone: 213-650-8000
Website: www.engrsnd.com
Degrees/Certificate: Recording
Engineering Certificate (10-
month/720-clock hours program).

Canadian Schools

Recording Arts Canada, Ontario
PO Box 11025, 984 Hwy #8
Stoney Creek, Ontario, Canada
L8E 5P9
Phone: 888-662-2666
Website: www.recordingarts.com
Degrees/Certificate: Diploma in
Audio Engineering & Multimedia
Production (one-year program).

Recording Arts Canada, Quebec
34 Chemin des Ormes,
Ste-Anne-des-Lacs, Quebec, Canada
J0R 1B0
Phone: 514-224-8363
Website:
www.sympatico.ca/inst.enreg
Degrees/Certificate: Diplomas in
Audio Production and Computer-
Assisted Sound Design (one-year
programs).

The Banff Centre for the Arts
Box 1020 Station 28
Banff, Alberta, Canada T0L 0C0
Phone: 403-762-6180
Website:
www.banffcentre.ab.ca/music
Degrees/Certificate: Audio Assistant
and Associate Work/Study (one- to
three-term programs).

Trebas Institute, British Columbia
112 East 3rd Ave.
Vancouver, BC, Canada V5T 1C8
Phone: 604-872-2666
Website: www.trebas.com
Degrees/Certificate: Diplomas in
Audio Engineering, Recorded
Music Production, Music Business
Administration, Film/Television
Production, New Media
Development, and 3-D Animation
(one-year programs); Bachelor of
Arts Degrees in Sound Technology
(two-years, following one-year diplo-
ma in Audio Engineering (in partner-
ship with the Liverpool Institute for
Performing Arts).

glossary

Absolute Gain — The highest gain in volume achievable before feedback occurs.

Acoustics — The act or sense of hearing; or anything relating to producing, arising from, or carrying sound.

Amplifier — A device capable of increasing the power level, voltage or current of a signal. Amplifiers strengthen the audio signal to a level at which loudspeakers can operate with minimal distortion.

Attenuator — A device that trims, or reduces, the volume of a signal.

Background Noise — see *Noise*.

Balanced — As found in audio cables, a pair of conductors whose voltages are opposite in polarity but equal in magnitude. Balanced lines reduce interference from external sources because they are shielded by a third, surrounding conductor. Also see *Unbalanced*.

Bandwidth — The range of frequencies (from low to high) covered by audio devices.

Basket — The framework for all of the speaker's components. Most of the top-of-the-line models use an aluminum alloy for the basket. This material is lightweight and does not interfere with the movements of the speaker's magnet.

Bass — The low audio frequency range; approximately 400Hz and lower.

Bi-amped — A bi-amped audio system uses a crossover (active or passive) to divide a full range audio signal into two separate power amplifiers—one for the lows and one for the high frequencies.

Bridging — The connecting of one electrical circuit in parallel with another.

Capacitance — A property that permits the storage of electricity when a potential difference exists between the conductors.

Capacitor — An electronic device that passes AC currents and blocks DC currents. A capacitor is also used to store voltage.

Cardioid — A microphone with a "heart-shaped" pick-up pattern. This type of microphone is more sensitive to sound projected to its front than its back, and is good for feedback rejection.

Channel Equalizer — The part of a sound mixer used to boost or attenuate certain frequencies on each of a mixer's channels.

Clipping — The distortion of an audio signal that occurs when the abilities of an amplifier are exceeded.

Coloration — Audible alterations arising from the response pattern of a microphone or loudspeaker; also indicates alterations to the sound of the environment in question.

Compression Driver — A high frequency transducer that uses a diaphragm (instead of a cone) coupled to a horn, thus making it more efficient in radiating sound into the air. Used for emitting mid- and high-range frequencies.

Compressor — An amp that decreases its gain as the level of an input signal increases. It may operate over the range of inputs, or only on signals above or below a given level, or threshold.

Condenser Microphone — A microphone that uses a capacitor as a pick-up element, and requires phantom power (48 volts) to operate. The output from a condenser microphone is usually higher than that of dynamic microphones.

Conductor — A substance, usually metal, that permits the free flow of electrons.

Cone — The vibrating diaphragm found in some speakers that generates sound waves.

Cone Driver — A driver that employs a cone attached to a voice coil. Cone drivers are less efficient than compression drivers.

Crossover — A device that separates an audio signal into two or more frequency ranges, which can make a PA more efficient by having separate amplifiers power each frequency range. There are active and passive crossovers.

Current — The rate of flow of electricity in a circuit.

Cut-off Frequency — The highest or lowest frequency in the pass band or filter.

Decibel (dB) — The unit of measurement that describes the ratio between true power, voltage, or sound pressure levels. Zero dB is the threshold of human hearing, with 1 dB representing the smallest change in volume perceptible to humans. The unit used to measure sound levels.

Decay — The fading of a sound after its initial attack.

Delay — A device that delays an audio signal; commonly used to repeat an audio signal.

Diaphragm —The part of a dynamic loudspeaker attached to the voice coil that produces sound when moved. Usually formed in the shape of a cone or a dome.

Direct (DI) Box — An interface device used to convert high-impedance, unbalanced output from instruments, amplifiers, etc. into low-impedance, balanced microphone output for input at the mixer.

Distortion — Any change in an audio signal that causes a waveform to appear differently at the output than at the input.

Driver — A loudspeaker unit consisting of the electromagnetic components of a speaker, typically a magnet and a voice coil, that feeds sound pressure waves into the horn.

Dropout — A loss of signal.

Dust Cover/Cap — Protects the voice coil of a speaker from dust and dirt. It is usually made from paper, plastic, or aluminum.

Dynamic Microphone — A microphone that converts acoustic energy to electrical energy through a moving coil around a fixed magnet.

Dynamic Range — The difference between the loudest and quietest performances during a musical presentation, as perceived by human ears. Measured in decibels.

Electromagnetic Energy — Electrical energy, or current, that is generated when a conductor is displaced, or moves, within a magnetic field.

Electronic Coloration — See *Coloration*.

Electrostatic Energy — Energy produced by conductive electrical charge, instead of motion.

Enclosure — A housing structure acoustically designed to hold a speaker or speakers.

Equalization — The increasing or decreasing of frequency ranges through the use of tone controls, equalizers or filters.

Equalizer (EQ) — A signal-processing device that adjusts the tone, or frequency response, of a signal. Found on mixers, channels, or outboard processors.

Fader — Either a rotary dial or slider that serves as the master volume control for the signal delivered to the output groups for each channel of a sound mixer.

Feedback — The regeneration of a signal from the output that reenters the input, creating a loop that can cause a squealing sound.

Filter — Any electrical circuit or mechanical device that removes or attenuates energy at certain frequencies.

Frequency — Changes in sound, proportional to the number of waveforms that repeat in a given period. Measured in Hertz (Hz). Also used to describe musical pitch: the lower the frequency, the lower the pitch.

Frequency Response — The range of frequencies that a device will produce or reproduce; usually 20–20,000 Hz.

Gain — An increase of signal strength or signal level delivered to a channel preamp; also the control that increases or decreases a signal's level.

Gain-Before-Feedback — The amount of headroom a sound system has before the output level becomes great enough to introduce feedback.

Gain Structure — The interconnectedness of audio equipment components, and the amount of amplification and attenuation that is performed by each component. Gain structure is crucial to optimization of dynamic range and signal-to-noise ratio throughout the sound system.

Graphic Equalizer — An equalizer with multiple controls, or bands, that control set frequencies. Changes the relative levels of frequencies.

Harmonic Frequency — Frequency derived from integral multiple(s) of the fundamental—or first harmonic—frequency, i.e. the second harmonic is twice the fundament frequency, the third harmonic is three-times the fundamental frequency, etc.

Harmonic/Ghost Tone — Forms of unwanted distortion. Also see *Total Harmonic Distortion* (THD).

Headroom — The capacity of a device above its normal operating level in which it can permit peaks to pass undistorted.

Hertz (Hz) — Units, in cycles per second. Used to measure frequency.

Horn — A device coupled to a driver; used to project sound more efficiently.

Hypercardioid — A microphone pick-up pattern shaped like a "figure-eight," with an even narrower pick-up pattern than the supercardioid, and capable of stronger sound pick-up at the rear of the microphone.

Impedance — The degree to which a circuit impedes, or resists, the flow of current; measured in ohms. Most speakers are rated at 8 ohms. High-impedance microphones are rated at 10,000+ ohms, and low-impedance microphones at 50–250 ohms.

Input — The section of a mixer that receives the signal from the microphone, effects processor, amplifier, or loudspeaker.

Input Level — The acceptable operating input of a device.

Interference — A disturbance, usually from another transmitting device (such as a television or radio station), that obstructs, interrupts, or degrades signal transmission.

Jack — The connection point for a cable's plug.

Lavalier — Small microphones wired to a mini body-pack transmitter; usually clipped onto the neck or chest area. Because of their inconspicuous and unobtrusive design, Lavalier microphones are often used in television broadcast.

LED (Light Emitting Diode) — A device used to indicate signal level.

Line Level — An input or output pre-amplified signal, in contrast to microphone level. Actual signal levels vary, with the nominal mic level being –50dB and nominal line level being +4dB.

Loudness — The sound level as perceived by human ears.

Low-frequency Roll-off — The attenuation that occurs at the lower or upper frequency range of a driver, network, or system.

Magnet — A speaker component. The size of a speaker's magnet determines the strength of the magnetic field generated by that speaker (i.e. the larger the magnet, the more efficient the speaker). Because efficiency is related to magnet size, the more efficient and top-of-the-line speakers usually cost more.

Masking — A unique situation where one or more sounds can trick the ear into not hearing sounds that is simultaneously present.

Mixer — A device that brings together audio signals to be leveled, manipulated, and processed before being sent to power amplifiers and speakers.

Moving Coil Microphone — One of the two types of dynamic microphones.

Noise — Any unwanted or unnatural signal in an audio mix: hiss, hum, etc.

Omnidirectional — A microphone pick-up pattern with a 360-degree pick-up radius; it is capable of picking up sound evenly in all directions.

Pad — A network of resistors that are used to decrease the input of a signal; used to prevent signal overload.

Pan — A procedure used to redirect an audio signal. In a stereo system, it is the ability to send a signal to the left or right.

Parametric EQ — An equalizer with separate controls for frequency, bandwidth, and boost/cut. It also includes a Q for bandwidth adjustment. Unlike a Peaking EQ, which covers the area of an octave, the Q control can narrow or broaden that bandwidth which gives greater control over changing the signal.

Peaking EQ — An equalizer with a selectable bandwidth that will either boost or cut a certain number of decibels around a center frequency. This type of EQ is most commonly used to change mid-frequencies.

Phantom Power — The operating voltage supplied by a mixer or external power source.

Phase — Describes the relationship between two or more waves and how they affect one another.

Piezo — A type of crystal that vibrates when voltage is applied to it. Used to reproduce high frequencies in speaker cabinets.

Pitch — The perceived frequency of a sound.

Preamp — A device that amplifies, or increases, the volume of a low or line level signal.

Proximity Effect — An increase in low frequency, or bass, response when a microphone is in close proximity to the source.

Q — A tone control that has the ability to broaden or narrow its bandwidth.

Real Time Analyzer (RTA) — A device that electronically uses a display to show the energy level of all frequencies present.

Receiver — A device that picks up radio signals from a transmitter and converts to audio signals.

Resistor — A device that offers resistance to the flow of both AC and DC current.

Response Pattern — The way in which a microphone accentuates or de-emphasizes particular frequencies.

Reverb — The continuation of a sound after the initial attack. Reverb is created by sound waves bouncing off of reflective services, such as walls, floors, etc.; an effect that can be recreated by spring or electronic devices.

Ribbon Microphone — One of two types of dynamic microphones.

Roll-off — The reduction of signal level as the frequency of the signal moves away from the cut-off frequency, especially when the cut-off rate is mild.

Shelving EQ — A type of equalizer which, when boosted, forms a frequency response curve which looks like a shelf.

Signal-to-Noise Ratio — The ratio of the average signal to the background noise. Measured in decibels.

Sine Wave — The fundamental wave from a pure audio tone; a wave with no harmonics.

Slew Rate — The ability of an amplifier to follow a fast-rising waveform. The faster the slew rate, the better.

Sound Pressure Level (SPL) — A measurement of sound energy; usually measured in dB.

Sound Pressure Wave — A wave from a sound source. The ears physically respond to the variations in the pressure.

Spider — A speaker component that connects the cone to the basket. The spider is made with pleats, or folds, that allow the pumping action of the speaker to occur without causing any undo stress to the cone.

Supercardioid — A microphone pick-up pattern similar to that of a cardioid, but more narrow, and capable of some sound pick-up at the rear of the microphone.

Threshold of Pain — Sound pressure levels at or exceeding 130 dB SPL.

Timbre — The quality of a sound related to its harmonic structure. It is the aspect of a voice or instrument that gives it its sonic signature, i.e. why a flute and a trumpet sound different when they play the same note.

Total Harmonic Distortion (THD) — Audible distortion produced by a power amplifier when at full power; caused by a small variance between the output and input signals. Also see *Harmonic/Ghost Tones*.

Transducer — A device that converts input energy into output energy of another form, i.e. acoustic to electric.

Transmitter — A device that converts an audio signal into a radio signal that is broadcast through an antenna, ultimately to be picked up by a receiver.

Tri-amping — A system utilizing a three-way crossover and three individual power amps. The full-range signal is divided into three frequency ranges by the crossover, and its own amplifier increases each range

Trim — A device that trims, or reduces, the volume of a signal. Also see *Attenuator*.

Tweeter — A component in speaker cabinets designed to reproduce high frequencies.

UHF — Acronym for the ultra-high frequency range of the radio spectrum, extending from 300 MHz to 3 GHz. Used extensively in satellite communication and broadcasting.

Unbalanced — As found in audio cables, consisting of one conductor and a shield, which also carries the other half of the signal. More prone to interference than a balanced line. Also see *Balanced*.

Vent — The opening in the back of the magnet assembly, that allows for the release of pressure built up by the moving of the voice coil under the dust cover/cap.

VHF — Acronym for the very high frequency range of the radio spectrum, extending from 30 MHz to 300 MHz (thus longer than UHF waves). Used extensively with two-way mobile radio communications.

Voice Coil — A wire—usually made of copper or aluminum—that winds around a cylinder made of plastic, paper, or aluminum. Since copper is a better conductor than aluminum, it is often favored in speaker design.

Volume — A term used to describe the level of signal or the intensity of a sound.

Watts — A unit of measure for electrical or acoustic power.

XLR — The type of connector most commonly used for microphone cables. This type of connector is popular because it locks into place and cannot be unplugged accidentally.